A COMPLETE SYSTEM OF
CATHOLIC EDUCATION IS NECESSARY

A COMPLETE SYSTEM OF CATHOLIC EDUCATION IS NECESSARY

by
ROY J. DEFERRARI, Ph. D.
The Catholic University of America

A reply to

"Are Parochial Schools the Answer?"
by Mary Perkins Ryan

ST. PAUL EDITIONS

NIHIL OBSTAT:

REVEREND HARRY A. ECHLE

Censor Librorum

IMPRIMATUR:

✠ PATRICK A. O'BOYLE, D.D.

Archbishop of Washington

The *nihil obstat* and *imprimatur* are official declarations that a book or pamphlet is free of doctrinal or moral error. No implication is contained therein that those who have granted the *nihil obstat* and the *imprimatur* agree with the content, opinions, or statements expressed.

Library of Congress Catalog Card Number: 64-22429

Printed by the *Daughters of St. Paul*
50 St. Paul's Ave., Jamaica Plain
Boston, Mass. 02130

CONTENTS

Part I

The Nature of
Catholic Education 13

Part II

Mrs. John Julian Ryan
and Catholic Education 33

Preface

Much criticism of the Catholic Educational System has appeared in print in the United States during the last decade, and, all things considered, much good should be derived from it. However, in all this discussion, there appears a trend away from certain fundamental principles which have guided Catholic Education in our country throughout its history, and which many of us feel should always be kept in mind for the general good. It is the purpose of this book to review these principles.

Very recently there has appeared a book by Mary Perkins Ryan, which has caused a great disturbance among the reading portion of our Catholic population. It is entitled: "Are Parochial Schools the Answer? Catholic Education in the Light of the Council," New York, 1964. This work is extremely critical of all American Catholic Education, and, unfortunately, is based on several misconceptions. Accordingly, it is our purpose also to analyze this work.

PART I

THE NATURE OF
CATHOLIC EDUCATION

THE NATURE
OF
CATHOLIC EDUCATION

Before anyone attempts to consider the nature of Catholic education, he must establish for himself what the important aims of Catholic education are. Much has been written on this topic, but, unfortunately, entirely too frequently much less has been done in an effort to implement the theory. Every academic institution in the land is called upon, again and again, to express its aims either in its various publications, such as the catalogue and other official literature, or in the public utterances of its administrators. These expressions of opinion are, all in all, extremely well formulated. They can be set forth glibly by all connected with the institution—members of the faculty, administration, and the student body. But the fact that these aims have been carefully worked out and thoroughly absorbed by all concerned is no guarantee that they are being accomplished.

When presenting the aims of a Catholic school, almost invariably Pope Pius XI, in his encyclical **The Christian Education of Youth,** is quoted at least in part as follows: "Christian education takes in the whole aggregate of human life, physical and spiritual, intellectual and moral, individual, domestic, and social, not with a view to reducing it in any way, but in order to elevate, regulate, and perfect it, in accordance with the example and teaching of Christ.

"Hence, the true Christian, the product of Christian education, is the supernatural man who thinks, judges, and acts constantly, consistently in accordance with the example and teaching of Christ; in other words, to use the current term, the true and finished man of character."

This statement is, of course, very general and would never completely satisfy an accrediting agency or any serious evaluating group.

The following are a set of aims established by Sister Emmanuel Collins, O.S.F., for St. Teresa's College, Winona, Minnesota, on which, I think, all Catholic educators would agree. They are applicable, not only to the

Catholic college, but they cannot be completely ignored by any phase of Catholic education, if the term "Catholic" is to have any appreciable significance.

"To produce the true and finished man of character, the man who has

1. The sound knowledge of Catholic theology basic to the formation of the Christian character;

2. A 'philosophic mind' with habits of intellectual curiosity, discriminating inquiry, and precision;

3. The ability to speak, read, write, and listen intelligently;

4. An understanding and appreciation of his cultural heritage;

5. An understanding of the physical world around him;

6. A knowledge of Christian principles and attitudes toward man as a social and political being; and

7. A sound knowledge and proper habits of physical and mental health."

If the aims of Catholic education generally and higher education in particular, as just stated, are for the most part acceptable, we are ready to proceed. Before doing so, however,

17

it should be stated that only in recent years have our Catholic school administrators in any great numbers been stating their aims with any detail. Only when the accrediting agencies, a little less than fifty years ago, demanded that every institution wishing to be approved by them declare their aims, did they do so in great numbers. It is shocking to realize that some of them, when faced with this necessity were very inept in doing so. Only recently, the aims of a small institution were brought to my attention which included all aims except those of the mind and the intellect, namely, the religious, social, physical, and cultural, but not the basic training of the mind. This, of course, is playing into the hands of some non-Catholic and unfriendly critics who insist that Catholics, in all their educational thinking, are concerned with one thing only, that their children be taught religion well. Their opinion will certainly not be changed at all by reading Mrs. Mary Perkins Ryan's most recent book: "Are Parochial Schools the Answer?" This phase represents probably the first problem of Catholic education, the proper understanding of all the aims and the real place of the intellectual training among these. It should, of course, hold first place carefully joined with all the rest, but subordinate to none. This is the primary job of an academic institution.

In the implementation of Catholic education, the all-important problem is obtaining enough properly trained teachers. This involves much more than appears evident at first sight. The teachers must be able to teach their subjects in a manner that will place them in their proper perspective with all the other subjects of the curriculum. They must be able to integrate as they teach. When they fail to do so, they presumably teach with no thought of making the knowledge thus imparted of any direct value in the lives of their students. They teach their respective subjects solely for the sake of the subjects themselves; they are subject-centered, not student-centered. It is not surprising then that a United States Commissioner of Education some years ago became greatly concerned with such a serious weakness and went to what seems to some of us, as Catholic educators, to be the opposite extreme, the reform of all public school education around a core of vocational subjects. Preparation for life through formal education was viewed in the most practical and functional way.

All this is, of course, illustrative of a kind of integration with which we would be willing to agree within reasonable limits. Certainly, in the teaching of Latin, those elements that relate to our own language and the various influences of Latin culture on our own contemporary civilization should be carefully and frequently pointed out. And teachers of mathematics should avoid purely theoretical problems, such as those involving the speed of a hare and a turtle or the distribution of a small plot of land which, after its division, would not provide sufficient space upon which to place the very smallest of buildings. Most of us would be willing to assert that, in due proportion, integration with life is necessary for good teaching in any field. But it is at this point that the secular and the Catholic educator come to the parting of the ways.

The secular educator is quite satisfied with a fair amount of success in achieving integration with life and would probably seek no further integration, if, indeed, he is aware of the existence or desirability of any other. The true Catholic educator cannot be satisfied with this alone. Indeed, if he stops here, his educational institution will be little different from the secular. He must seek integration through theology, under whatever name theology may raise her head in a Catholic school or college. In other words, the Catholic teacher must seek integration with the life of the next world as well as with life in the present, since the two are integrally related, and are essentially one.

It seems to me that this is the answer to the question which Mrs. Ryan raises. Only by the application of the Catholic philosophy of education systematically and completely from the beginning to the very end of a person's growth as a human being can he best achieve the true end of Catholic education. When we speak of the Catholic philosophy of education, we do not, of course, leave out the place of the home and parents in carrying out this important work, but we certainly do not eliminate entirely or in part the indispensable role of the Catholic school.

The following is a recent statement quite appropriate at this stage of our presentation: "Truth, no doubt, has unity, and man in his striving for knowledge and truth is driven by a desire for synthesis and unity. Truth and unity, says St. Thomas, are two interchangeable concepts. For to understand, to comprehend,

21

means to discover interconnection and order, to reduce multiple data to a unity of order.

"But this unity of the truth which always remains more an ideal of man than an achieved result, must not make us forget the multiplicity of diverse levels or realms of truth. For instance, we may distinguish the truth of the every-day practical world, the truth of modern positive science, the truth pursued by philosophy and the truth we attain and cherish as religious faith." [1]

This concept of integration, based on the acceptance of the fact that all knowledge is a single unit and that it can only be a unit if there is a central, unifying force, is no twentieth century idea. St. Augustine said:

"There is an immutable truth embracing all things that are true; a truth you cannot call yours, or mine, or any man's, but which is present to all who discern the things that are immutably true, as a light which in some miraculous way is both secret and yet open to all." [2] St. Thomas also speaks often of the "oneness of truth" and of man's unified nature, so that the process of true learning requires an integrating and ordered relationship among the various disciplines, all subordinated to man's ultimate end. The true Catholic educator has always recognized this basic unity of knowledge and the need of synthesis in a Christian education, and he has been blessed with the only existing successful means of integration by reason of his unhesitating confidence in the truths of the theology and the philosophy which he professes. Many non-Catholics envy us this priceless possession; many of them also would gladly adopt our theology and philosophy for the purpose, at least, of achieving the integration and the unity in their teaching which is so necessary if the educational product is to be the integrated man. Because they may not use the name of God in the classroom and may not use principles of thinking to which sectarian significance may be attached, they must confine themselves to a social philosophy involving only the affairs of the world.

To implement successfully the Catholic concept of integration more is needed than the mere introduction into the program, of courses in theology and religion, philosophy and Church history, important as these contributions are to the student's overall education. The ultimate objectives of these courses and the ultimate objective of the total program must pentrate every teaching field of the school or college. Courses in theology, philosophy, and, to a much less extent, history contain the tangible material by which the unification of all other fields may be brought about. Thus, these basic subjects, in addition to their own intrinsic value, must seep through all other subjects and serve as the pivotal and unifying factors of Catholic education. I do not hesitate to say that thus far in the United States this has not been done very successfully. This is the great challenge to Catholic educators in general today.

Unfortunately, this integration of which we speak, in a Catholic college program of study is not easy to achieve, and there are many obstacles put in the way of our achieving it, sometimes by Catholics themselves, even some in high places. In our efforts to maintain our Catholic school system in its entirety, many difficulties arise to plague us. The financial cost involved is great, indeed, but we believe that, if Catholics stick to their principles, a satisfactory solution to this problem will eventually be reached.

Any move, however, that will break the solid line of Catholic education from the beginning through the area of higher education is extremely harmful to our purposes. Our very purposes themselves are admittedly difficult to attain. Of course, they may be attained to some degree of excellence by students attending Catholic institutions only in part, but the excellence of the final product is bound to be affected to some extent, and a serious risk is undergone by those concerned. Thus, while appreciating the sincerity and good will of those who suggest plans involving attendance at Catholic schools only in part, I cannot go along with them, at least in theory. Our youngsters need all the exposure to Catholic education, as I have described it above, that they can get. I cannot sympathize, except as a temporary measure, with plans such as those of "Shared Time"; the elimination of the early grades, even up to the college, possibly doing away even with all Catholic instruction except higher education; or the reverse of this, the retention of the early grades only, on the principle given us by psychologists that the earliest years of a child's life are the most impressionable. I do, however, strongly believe in cooperation, not elimination, between Catholic educational institutions and, rarely, under very extraordinary circumstances, with non-Catholic schools and colleges.

I have yet to see any serious criticism of Catholic education in its theory, or in the presentation of its ideal. The complaints arise over local conditions or certain difficulties as widespread as in an entire diocese. I might add also that they arise sometimes from unfortunate personal experiences. The great task which faces all Catholic educators is to work together steadily and courageously, so as to improve Catholic education and to bring it ever closer to the ideal. The chief obstacles, especially in the way of doing this in higher education, are, in my opinion, as follows.

There is the difficulty of establishing and maintaining a well trained faculty, one which is itself truly integrated intellectually and thus able to teach with proper integration. Those in high places are naturally eager to spread the influence of Catholic education as widely as possible and as quickly as possible. Thus, they place unreasonable demands on those who are responsible for furnishing the necessary and properly trained teachers. They do not seem to realize the nature of this training and the time required to bring it about effectively.

PART I

The superiors of religious communities feel obliged to yield to those requests and postpone or abandon plans for the continued training of their subjects. The superiors themselves are not always without blame in this problem. They often demand, for one reason or another, unreasonably heavy teaching loads and additional subsidiary duties of the teachers, and thus fail to give them time to read and study and even to do a little research in their field of specialization. Thus, the weakness in faculty training is reflected much more than many realize in the criticism of Catholic education. An old friend of mine, who had sent his children regularly to Catholic schools, finally came to the parting of the ways. He had enrolled one of his boys in a Catholic high school, when suddenly this institution, by an ill-advised order of higher authority, changed its program of studies from a general one, training for college as well as for immediate entry into the world, to a strictly terminal program, that is, training directly for the business world. My friend became furious and rightly so, and he transferred his son to a public high school, but I could not agree with him on the terrible things that he said about Catholic education in general. His accusations were justified insofar as they referred to his particular experiences, not as applied to the entire philosophy of Catholic education.

Because Catholic education lacks religious teachers in sufficient numbers, it must employ many secular persons, which in itself is highly desirable, if the proper personnel is available. But this leads directly into the problem of money. Unless the directors of Catholic higher education have the funds to pay these lay teachers salaries comparable to some degree with those which they can demand in secular institutions, they will have to employ inferior laymen, which naturally leads to more justifiable criticism.

I mentioned above the importance of Catholic teachers in higher education having enough time to do a little research. In spite of what some administrators and teachers themselves say to the contrary, this is quite necessary for the kind of teaching which we laymen expect our children to receive when we send them to Catholic educational institutions. But the fact remains that research activity is not encouraged in most of our Catholic institutions of higher education, to say nothing of those on lower levels. It is for the most part ignored. The religious are busy with less important things around the college and the convent, and laymen will insist on time within which to do this work and demand lighter teaching loads, and, if successful in their projects, even more salary. More serious even than this is reflected in the open action of a Catholic college faculty taken recently to the effect that it did not regard research of any serious importance for the teacher. Furthermore, it voted that research, unless dealing with problems in teaching itself, was not desireable. I have my own explanation of this attitude. The Sister members of the faculty, most of whom did not possess the doctorate, were content with a day-to-day routine performance of their duties, in which they did not wish to be disturbed, and the laymen were simply inferior intellectually and could not do any worthwhile scientific investigation even if they had the opportunity. I dare say that, if the number of anti-intellectuals on our small Catholic college faculties could be determined, it would be a real scandal and a shock to us all. Many Catholic laymen today are aware of the intellectual stagnation in so many of our schools, including small colleges and even in some of the larger ones. Not many years ago, a Catholic laywoman came to me for advice on where to send her daughter to college. I at once recommended several Catholic colleges for women in her general area. "But," she said, "I want to send her to a college with a strong faculty, where she will come in contact with genuine scholars of national and even world reputations," and she mentioned several non-Catholic institutions, also in her area, which had that kind of a faculty. Some may ask: "Doesn't this all go back ultimately to the financial problem?" It does to a great degree, of course. But it seems to me to be linked with at least one other basic cause. It appears to denote a lack of sound leadership in the institution concerned. Granted that it is due chiefly to a lack of funds, administrators should, nevertheless, struggle to meet the difficulty. I am confident that help will come to us from one source or another, if we do not completely abandon all hope.

Some administrators in complete despair over all these troubles think nothing of hiring non-Catholics as teachers, if they can procure their services at low enough salaries. How they can expect to carry on a program of integrated studies with such a policy as this is difficult to understand. Morever, this tendency toward a feeling of futility on the part of our Catholic educational leaders in meeting such problems and settling for whatever is easiest for them to achieve, if allowed to continue to spread, will do untold harm to Catholic education.

All of us interested in this work of Catholic education, especially higher education, and those assigned to the terrific task of implementing it, must, I repeat, stick everlastingly to the job. We must not relax even a little in our principles. In fact, genuine progress is being made today, but obstacles are unwittingly being raised against us by some of our own from whom we would normally expect encouragement and help.

NOTES TO PART I

[1] Albert Dondayne, *Faith and the World, Duquesne Studies: Theological Series I* (Pittsburgh, Pa.: Duquesne University Press, 1963), p. 181.

[2] St. Augustine, *On Free Will,* 2.12.33.

MRS. JOHN JULIAN RYAN
AND
CATHOLIC EDUCATION

MRS. JOHN JULIAN RYAN
AND
CATHOLIC EDUCATION

The recent appearance of Mrs. Ryan's book, "Are Parochial Schools the Answer?" has created a tremendous furor in Catholic educational circles. It has, indeed, brought out into the open many varied opinions about, not only the parochial schools, but Catholic education as it exists on all levels. The weakness of all the discussion that has come forth seems to me to lie in what appears to be a complete lack of any understanding of what true Catholic education (which I have attempted to summarize in Part I) really is and to be centered entirely on the problems concerned with carrying it on. In other words, the difficulties and failures of Catholic education have been identified with Catholic education itself. This, it seems to me, is a very unfortunate and dangerous trend. Admittedly, Catholic education has some serious problems to face, the least of which is not the financial one. The problem of procuring properly trained personnel to carry it on, teachers and administrators, at first glance seems even greater. But if we truly believe in the philosophy of Catholic education as I have attempted to describe it above, we should by no means think of abandoning it to any extent. We should keep it and promulgate it, and carry it on as fully as circumstances permit, always looking forward to extending it as our resources allow. I would say that the greatest mistake which has been made thus far has been to over-extend our efforts and to attempt to carry out our ideas on Catholic education sometimes with inferior teachers and equipment, placing our confidence in a principle commonly expressed in the statement: "Any Catholic school, regardless of its defects, is better than any non-Catholic school, regardless of its excellence." I recall with horror visiting a Catholic high school of a large eastern city in which I found extremely large laboratories being used as classrooms, and an atrociously large number of students under a single teacher in a number of individual classes. When I asked the reasons for this condition, I received a frank answer: "We have been ordered not to refuse the admission to our high school of any Catholic child who may apply." Much of this sort of thing can be discovered and rightly criticized, but we must not permit it to tear us from our moorings. Because of the great interest stirred up by Mrs. Ryan's book, and since it includes so many of the common criticisms of Catholic education, I would like to make some comments which I have jotted down as I have read the work carefully from beginning to end.

Certainly, Mrs. Ryan has the right to express her own views on the importance of parochial schools and Catholic education. Moreover, I would defend that right to the very end. I may have different views on many aspects of this great question, but, by the same token, I have a right to express them. I wish to take advantage of this right in this book.

There are two general errors which constantly come to the fore throughout the book. One of these we have adverted to several times already, Mrs. Ryan's failure to understand fully the nature and importance of academic integration. Academic integration, as we have attempted to describe it, is the great differentiating factor in Catholic education. Moreover, it includes religious education, if I understand Mrs.

37

Ryan's description of it, but the latter cannot stand alone. General education, which she appears to consider of minor importance, is held together and unified by religious education. Catholic education, properly conceived and carried out, is held together as a compact unit, as great educators long before our time have recognized. [1] Even in recent times, we have the non-Catholic, Robert Hutchins, once the Chancellor of the University of Chicago, calling our attention, again and again to the great blessing that we Catholics have in the recognition of the binding force of theology. Finally, we have Pius XI himself in his encyclical, **The Christian Education of Youth,** where he says: "The proper and immediate end of Christian education is to cooperate with divine grace in forming the true and perfect Christian, that is, to form Christ Himself in those regenerated by baptism ... **The mere fact that a school gives some religious instruction ... does not bring it into accord with the rights of the Church and the Christian family, or make it a fit place for Catholic students. To be this, it is necessary that all its teaching and the whole organization of the school and its teachers, syllabi, and textbooks in every branch, be regulated by the**

Christian spirit, . . . so that religion may be in very truth the foundation and crown of the youth's entire training." [2] It seems to me that we should recognize the importance of theology in any form of education worthy of the name of Catholic, and that this recognition should include its function as the great binding force of our educational system and not relegate it to an isolated position, however valuable the subject in itself may be.

In this connection, I would like to quote from **Pacem in Terris,** to which Mrs. Ryan refers occasionally in other connections:

"INTEGRATION OF FAITH AND ACTION

151. It is no less clear that today, in traditionally Christian nations, secular institutions, although demonstrating a high degree of scientific and technical perfection, and efficiency in achieving their respective ends, not infrequently are but slightly affected by Christian motivation or inspiration.

152. It is beyond question that in the creation of those institutions many contributed and continue to contribute who were believed to be and who consider themselves Christians; and without doubt, in part at least, they were

and are. How does one explain this? It is Our opinion that the explanation is to be found in an inconsistency in their minds between religious belief and their action in the temporal sphere. It is necessary, therefore, that their interior unity be re-established, and that in their temporal activity faith should be present.

"INTEGRAL EDUCATION

153. It is Our opinion, too, that the above-mentioned inconsistency between the religious faith in those who believe and their activities in the temporal sphere, results—in great part—from the lack of a solid Christian education. Indeed, it happens in many quarters and too often that there is no proportion between scientific training and religious instruction: the former continues and is extended until it reaches higher degrees, while the latter remains at elementary level. It is indispensable, therefore, that in the training of youth, education should be complete and without interruption, namely, that in the minds of the young religious values should be cultivated and the moral conscience refined in a manner to keep pace with the continuous and ever more abundant assimilation of scientific and technical knowledge. And it is indispens-

able, too, that they be instructed regarding the proper way to carry out their actual tasks."

The second general error, which crops up again and again, is an apparent lack of understanding on the part of Mrs. Ryan of the nature and methods of true scientific scholarship. While she quotes rarely, and then from secondary sources, her chief sources are her own experiences and conversations with certain consultants. Anything like a complete collection of primary source material, and a systematic organization of this information, followed by an objective appraisal of its significance, not a straining to exact support for preconceived notions, is completely lacking. The reader is left in great confusion at times by the lack of a logical sequence in the author's story. Certainly, any treatment of a subject so vital as that of the book before us should have the best logical scientific approach.

Obviously, Mrs. Ryan should have defined exactly what she meant by "religious education." While this can be surmised fairly well, yet one would feel much safer if he could be sure, through her own words, as to just what this is. In other words, just what is Mrs. Ryan's understanding of the Catholic philosophy of education? Is she critical of this or of the manner in which the educators in the United States have attempted to implement it? Or is religious education in her mind synonymous with religious formation, and is its aim "to make people more acceptable to God?" If our guess as to what Mrs. Ryan understands by religious education is correct, is the objective the same on any level of education, and are the steps to be taken to achieve it essentially the same throughout the system? Unless these questions are answered for the most part, it will be very difficult to discuss the content of her book thoroughly, except in piece-meal fashion. In any case, it is my purpose to discuss Mrs. Ryan's book as well as I can, section by section, and to conclude with a few general observations of my own in addition.

Mrs. Ryan feels that "from the older, conventional point of view still widely held today, our Catholic schools seem to be meeting these requirements of Pius XI by giving religious instruction and general education in a religious atmosphere." But academic integration involves much more than general education in a religious atmosphere. No serious educator ever feels that the requirements are being fully met.

42

There is much self-criticism in Catholic school circles.

A little later she says: "But the matter of this religious instruction is still, generally speaking, the questions and answers of the Baltimore Catechism, and the aim is still merely to fix the answers firmly in the children's memories." This is not the fault of the system. It is poor religion-teaching which exists in CCD as well as in the Catholic school. It is gradually being changed wherever religion is being taught, but, naturally, the progress is slow. It is, however, definitely being felt in the Catholic school system and not only in catechetics elsewhere. But she adds that "from the point of view of the catechetical renewal which has slowly been gaining ground over the last decades, it appears certain that the whole question of the objectives, the content, and the manner of religious instruction needs to be thought out afresh." Now what does she mean by "religious instruction"; the teaching of religion or perhaps Catholic education generally? A rapid glance at the contents of our professional educational journals will show that no subject receives so much attention by scholars as to the method of presentation as religion, or theology, or what have you. In fact, editors of these periodicals will tell you that they are already literally embarrassed by a plethora of this material, including that from the point of view of the catechetical renewal. Any stimulus to greater activity along this line is hardly needed today.

To achieve the aims of Catholic education as expressed by the Holy Father, much more is needed than a thorough teaching of religion. Within each classification (pre-elementary, elementary, intermediate, secondary, and higher), all the aims and especially the real place of the intellectual training among these must be thoroughly understood. Intellectual training should, of course, hold first place, carefully integrated with all the rest to form the desired Catholic educational unit, but it should be subordinate to none. This is the primary job of any educational institution.

Mrs. Ryan says very appropriately that the problems involved in forming the true and perfect Christian, forming Christ Himself in young people, are so serious that they ought, surely, to be engaging the best minds and major efforts in every institution and in all of our educational organizations; that those chosen to

44

teach religion in high schools and colleges ought to be the cream of the teaching staff; that in the elementary schools, where one teacher handles many subjects, each teacher ought to have had at least as much training in how to teach religion as in how to teach, say, arithmetic or geography. With this probably everyone would agree and they would probably be willing to apply the same thoughts to all levels of Catholic education, except for the fact that with her the curriculum is evidently concerned primarily with religion and the importance of the unified program is lost.

It seems to me also that the tie-up of our educational problems today with the Ecumenical Council and the **aggiornamento** is a bit strained. Whether one agrees with the results or not, the rethinking and studying of educational procedures among Catholics in the United States has been very active for many years. Any awakening to a restudy of their problems in the light of present-day conditions is always necessary, but no more important than it is in other phases of Catholic life. To accept the thought of a special reawakening in the face of the facts would be to insinuate that the tremendous efforts of American Catholic educators over the last fifty years have been on the wrong track and with this I cannot agree.

In spite of the title of the book, the author makes an occasional remark by which she shows that she has in mind other levels of education than the parochial schools. For example, on pages 12 and 13, she says: "But there remains the all-important question of whether or not such a formation (i.e., Catholic) is actually being given in Catholic schools and colleges—a question that does not appear to have engaged the attention of the great majority of those responsible for the Catholic educational system." This causes confusion because the particular problem under discussion would need different treatment at the various levels of education. Furthermore, the last portion of the quotation does **not** appear to be true. At least in the field of higher education, I speak from long, direct experience and insist that it is **not** true. Details to the contrary can easily be given.

Indeed, to say that this question does not appear to have engaged the attention of the great majority of those responsible for the Catholic educational system, would, did I not know Mrs. Mary Perkins Ryan, be regarded as a deliberate insult to Catholic educators.

Again, Mrs. Ryan says: "The notion prevails, among Catholics and non-Catholics alike, that elementary schools, high schools, and colleges under Catholic auspices are an essential aspect of Catholic life, and that belief in the necessity of a Catholic educational system is almost an article of Catholic faith." Here, again, we have a great simplification of a problem. In spite of the preaching of many clergymen who have emphasized this aspect of the matter, I do not believe that it has been assimilated by the great majority of the Catholic people in the literal sense in which it has sometimes been preached. My own feeling on the question, like that of Mrs. Ryan's is **not** based on objective factual information. Our thoughts on the matter are, at best, strong impressions.

Academic integration, as I have already indicated, is basic in genuine Catholic education. But what the author says (p. 18) in part on this subject is most distressing. "What 'integration' exists on this level (i.e., for the eight grades of elementary school) is mainly along the lines of stressing the Catholic pioneers in

47

American history, including 'Catholic words' in spelling lists, introducing priests and Sisters into the stories selected for readers, and asking arithmetic questions about how many Hail Marys would have been said by a class of thirty-five by the time they had recited three decades of the Rosary." Some of this very naive thinking I am afraid does exist, but I am, by no means, willing to believe that it is prevalent. Moreover, this is not true integration, but a distortion of it. There is much more good, solid integration as anyone will see who takes the trouble to examine the question systematically.

The author makes a great deal out of the tremendous cost of Catholic education in the United States in comparison with the actual achievement obtained. What we get for the money and energy expended is not worthy of carrying on Catholic education with the prevailing methods, she thinks. Here, again, she is lumping all Catholic education at all its various levels into a single mass, and giving her impressions. To me, the statistics are very encouraging. We are reaching more and more of our young people, and if we continue to face our problems intelligently, all will be progressively better.

48

PART II

To me, Chapter 2 causes more distress than any other portion of the book. The following statement by Mrs. Ryan illustrates rather well the general content of the chapter. "As the Christians of the early centuries could profit from the pagan education of their time, making their own contribution to human learning, communicating with their pagan neighbor —by means of a common vocabulary and common patterns of thought—and thus sharing the light of Christ with them, perhaps Christians could act in the same way today in regard to secular education and learning of our own age." This and other similar statements of this nature are literally most shocking.

The picture of the past as presented in Chapter 2, "Hints from History," is far too rosy. The extensive apologetic literature which flooded the intellectual world of the Fathers from the second century to the end of the patristic period, and even into early medieval times, did not stem from a feeling that "the Christians of the early centuries could profit from the pagan education of their time, making their own contribution to human learning, communicating with their pagan neighbor—by means of a common vocabulary and common

49

pattern of thought—thus sharing the light of Christ with them." Rather were the Christians, both Greek and Roman, greatly disturbed by the possibility of young Christians sharing the darkness of paganism with their non-Christian fellow citizens, just as many of us are today. Those familiar with the writings of the Christian leaders of this world need no further elucidation of this point. The several works such as St. Basil's treatise addressed to youths on the usefulness of Greek literature were written to prevent a complete disregard in Christian circles of the benefits to be derived from cultural contact with classical literature. In other words, the thinking was that much is to be gained by a careful study of pagan classical literature, but it is to be carried on with great caution. Whatever Mrs. Ryan's conclusions may be in support of her subject, it is difficult to see how she can draw any support for them from the early history of the Church.

May I presume to tell the reader that the era of the Greek and Latin Fathers has been my special field of study for fifty years, and I am today still Editorial Director of the Series of the Fathers of the Church, a work projected for one hundred volumes of which fifty have already appeared through the Catholic University of America Press. This roughly covers all the material of the Fathers in the strict sense of the term. Thus, I feel very close to the Fathers and, having read so much of their writings in the original, I feel something approximating a personal relationship with them. My feeling of dismay, then, on reading Chapter 2 may well be imagined.

Mrs. Ryan says in this Chapter: "But the instruction given in a catechetical school did not consist of a series of lessons designed to give an intellectual grasp on the truths of faith. Rather, it was the proclamation of God's great deeds throughout sacred history and an opening out of the Christian way of life." Granted that religious formation cannot and should not be solely intellectual, does that mean that it is not intellectual at all? Were not intellectual goals included in the aim of the early Church's catechesis? If not, it would seem that we are contradicting the Church's definitions on faith.

There are so many half-truths and examples of misplaced emphasis in Chapter 3 that it is difficult, indeed, to analyze it. We read in part that it is a common belief among Catholics that if the children were let go from our schools, we would soon have no Church left. Rather do we fear that if we permit our children to go to non-Catholic institutions, we will lose a very effective ally in the sound training of our youngsters in the Catholic way of life. It has been my experience that, not only Catholics lose their faith in non-sectarian institutions, but non-Catholics as well. The Lord, of course, works in wondrous ways, and I do not overlook the fact that religious vocations are fostered on secular campuses.

Mrs. Ryan says that there seems to be a feeling that the Catholic layman has no place of importance, regardless of his training, in the work of Catholic schools and colleges. This probably is based, she declares, on the common belief that the lay teacher, as an integral part of Catholic education, is a new concept and that, in a material way, there is little to attract a layman to this walk of life. Historically, however, the lay teacher is not a recent acquisition to Catholic education, either in the United States or in European countries, but he has always made a considerable contribution to the system. As the Catholic school system in the United States grew rapidly in the present century and schools became a part of parish activities under the parish priest, it is true, as Mrs. Ryan says, that the whole work of Catholic education came to be regarded as purely ecclesiastical by many, and that the impression was strengthened by the fact that in Catholic schools comparatively few lay teachers were employed. Again, as Mrs. Ryan indicates, pastors, religious teachers, and parents frequently adopted an attitude of regarding the lay teacher professionally as of a lower status than the religious teacher on the assumption that the religious state itself gives special competence to a teacher.

With the present tremendous need for lay teachers in the Catholic school system, Catholic educators are again actively recognizing the part that qualified lay teaching personnel can and should play in the total school system. They consider them a powerful means for implementing Pope Pius' call for "Catholic Action" on the part of the laity; a genuine force for good among youth as practical and realistic examples of general "goodness" in individuals who are very much a part of our modern world; a substantial contribution to teach more efficiently than religious in certain fields; a means of broadening a religious faculty and reducing provincialism; and, in a public relations role, the effective interpretation of Catholic education to a lay public and non-Catholic educators.

However, the financial problems involved in attracting qualified lay teachers are admittedly great and complex. The three major problems of the practical order for the laymen in Catholic schools are: salaries, fringe benefits, and conditions of service. Much progress has already been made in Catholic education toward meeting them. I cite specifically the Archdiocese of San Francisco, Archdiocese of Detroit, Archdiocese of Milwaukee, Archdiocese of Cincinnati, Diocese of Peoria, and the Diocese of Youngstown. [2]

On page 68 of her book, Mrs. Ryan states unequivocally that vocational guidance as given in most Catholic schools and colleges is little more than non-Catholic counseling, involving such questions as "What are your aptitudes, tests, and circumstances; in view of them in what kind of work will you be happiest and most successful?" She seems to imply that while "Catholic schools and colleges" give at least passing consideration to counseling of a non-religious nature, the religious aspects of this activity are carried on very deficiently. There are over 700 secondary Catholic schools and colleges affiliated with the Catholic University and our experiences with them give us quite a different picture. In the first place, a good program of vocational guidance is a part of the larger activity of both general guidance and counseling. Many Catholic institutions like to separate the religious aspects of this work from the rest because it often involves the confessional. But the point which I wish to make now is that the guidance and counseling that takes in the spiritual development of pupils is usually carried on very well. Our difficulties involve the activities of guidance and counseling which do **not** especially involve the spirit. Moreover, the passing reference to and description of so-called "non-Catholic counseling" is not just. It borders on the slanderous.

The author does, however, make some pertinent remarks in this chapter with reference to teaching religion and Christian formation which may well be beneficial in meeting some of the difficulties in this field. But we object strongly to generalization, such as I have indicated above, which certainly does not do justice to the educational activities which are going on in our schools and colleges today.

Chapter 4, "Who Needs Formation," is very interesting, indeed. The author comes to the conclusion that all of us need formation during our entire lives, and dwells on what appears to me to be obvious, that adults need to develop spiritually and must not pin-point any event in their lives, such as confirmation, as the terminal point of their religious formation. We have here a good argument for the maintenance of the entire Catholic educational system, from kindergarten through college.

The strongest argument for the continuous Catholic educational training is that spiritual development should keep pace with intellectual growth. The world is full of adults, essentially all of them from secular schools, whose development of the mind has been going on throughout the years of their entire lives, but whose understanding of the spiritual world is stunted, stopped very frequently when they left the environment of the Catholic school, obsessed with the thought that their spiritual growth was long since completed. Here, of course, is the great difference between the secular and the Catholic schools. The administrators of secular educational centers are slightly, or even entirely, unconcerned with the spiritual development of the individual. They are willing to take the word of Catholics that the matters of the spirit can be learned at home or somewhere outside the school. Let the school take care of the things of the mind, and the affairs of the spirit will be cared for in the home or perhaps elsewhere. The school itself need not worry about them. This is all more or less summed up by the rather large group of parents who say: "John is well trained in his religion through the influence of our home. I don't worry about his losing his faith. I want to be sure that he gets a good cultural training." But the whole man must be trained in all his ramifications. One may not get ahead of or fall behind another, and to achieve this end and acquire an all-round development in our youngsters, we need the cooperation of the Catholic education all the way. The secular institution will fall far short of the spiritual growth desired. In any case, to achieve this full development, we need not only the Catholic school, but the proper cooperation of Catholic parents.

We should point out at this point that formal adult education has an important part to play here. Indeed, the Catholic Educational System has done far too little to bring Catholic Adult Education into its proper place in the picture.

The material in Chapter 5 is very interesting, but I do not see anything in it which would make me look with favor on the abandonment of our parochial schools or any part of our Catholic educational system. Mrs. Ryan summarizes her Chapter 5, "New Vistas," by saying in part that the American Catholic was once imprisoned in the mentality of the siege, but that this need be so no longer, since the spirit of ecumenism has freed him of the fear of denominational hostility, and since, although he finds himself facing the danger of secularism, he finds this secularism so interwoven with genuine humanism as to call for the active presence of Christians in modern society. Here, again, I do not follow the author very easily. I fear that, as far as Catholic education is concerned, she is making much out of little. She makes a great deal out of the "mentality of the siege." For many years, I have represented The Catholic University of America at numerous non-sectarian educational meetings, and I myself and the several Catholic educators associated with me did not experience any derogatory feelings resulting from the mentality of the siege. Probably the most outstanding illustration of this is in the United States Education Mission to Japan which was established in 1945, and in which Monsignor Frederick G. Hochwalt and myself were the Catholic representatives. Certainly, Monsignor Hochwalt would agree with me that we were not handicapped in the least by "the mentality of the siege." I could give many other examples of my mingling with non-Catholic educators and serving as a representative of Catholicism and being treated in a most friendly and cooperative manner. Certainly, I myself did not feel in the least inhibited when stating my opinion frankly on whatever topic was under discussion.

In Chapter 6, "Fears—Realistic and Otherwise," the author gives her thought on the fears, both explicit and more or less hidden, which many of us are likely to hold concerning what she calls "the open, sacramental Catholicism proposed and diffused by the Council." These are all quite subjective, and with some of them, I would agree and with others disagree strongly, all admittedly quite subjectively on my own part. A few of the latter will be presented here.

The author says that there may be many who, if we changed our accustomed ways of praying, would fear that we would be deprived of the familiar sense of safety that those ways afforded us. I do not feel this way. I also do not believe that lay Catholics generally have had a tendency to think that religion is a part of life which they are content to leave mainly to the clergy. The "mentality of the siege" is brought up several times as responsible for a number of weaknesses in all Catholics, religious and lay, in dealing with problems of the Church, including Catholic education. Much of this material includes half-truths.

A beautiful section, among others, appears in this Chapter 6, at the bottom of page 125 and on 126. Mrs. Ryan says that what is needed above all, perhaps by both clergy and laity, is the sense of belonging to a Church which by the will of God is involved in history, progressing toward the perfection willed for it by Christ—the perfection which He will give it only at His return in glory. Etc., etc. Certainly, I can find nothing to disagree with in these concluding remarks of Chapter 6.

PART II

Chapter 7, "The Initial Effort," presents much of a spiritual nature. Would that it could all be carried out as Mrs. Ryan so vividly portrays! The central aim of the renewal, as she says, is the formation of a Catholic people so open to the formation given by Christ and the Holy Spirit in the Church that they are continually enabled more fully to "practice the truth in love." She recognizes the enormity of the task and realizes that it must take precedence for the present over every other work, all under the direction of the bishops. She then describes the new training necessary for all walks of Catholic life, and in particular for the members of the clergy, in order to make their own the new outlook in relation to Scripture, scriptural and liturgical theology, the liturgy, pastoral practice, ecumenism, and social action. The following question comes to mind: "Is it not being done to a great extent now, and if not, is it practicable?"

In Chapter 8, "With or Without a Catholic School System," Mrs. Ryan raises the question whether we can afford, when the need for the religious formation of the whole Catholic people is so great, to provide a general education for all or even a part of young people. Again, we have confusion here regarding religious formation and its relationship to a general education. Again, she says: "How many priests will it be able to spare for the work of general, as opposed to religious education." But they are both one. They cannot properly be separated. This fallacy runs all through this chapter.

Any cutting off of the teaching of religion from the regular program of the institution does not eliminate the need of integrated courses in the rest of the program!

If a serious effort were made, she says, to provide adequate liturgical and home formation, coupled with formal religious instruction, for all Catholics, in place of the attempt to maintain our present educational system, it is hard to see why there need be any fear of a decline in membership. The proportion, she says further, of practicing Catholics might, on the contrary, be expected to improve. This I definitely do not believe.

If we were thus to make outside-of-school formation and instruction the norm for young Catholics, the Catholic school would cease to be the presumed rule and become the recognized exception, she says. This, I say in all seriousness, may God forbid.

62

PART II

"In the context of the new outlook, two major conclusions would seem to be inevitable: first, that a truly Catholic formation for all young people is a real possibility if we use all the resources at our disposal; and second, that **a general education under Catholic auspices is no longer as necessary or even as desirable as in the past.** As things are, the maintenance of our Catholic school system—not to speak of its extension—takes up a large part of our available human resources, **resources now needed for urgent religious tasks.** Even if some form of public aid were to relieve us of part of the financial burden, should we, then, plan for the continued maintenance of our Catholic school system in the future?" To this, I answer, "By all means."

Chapter 9, "New Resources of the Church," as presented by Mrs. Ryan, should cause genuine alarm to all Catholics. It is based on the same fallacious understanding, which runs through the book, of what Catholic education really is.

"Think, too, of the buildings which might now become parish centers or **schools of religion, or serve some other community purpose.**" Etc., etc.

According to Mrs. Ryan in Chapter 10, "A New Climate in the Church," the Church has existed intent on self-preservation, spending its efforts to hold its own, to preserve, to fight off attacks, to centralize authority, and to maintain order within the ranks; that in such a climate it does not seem to matter very much what a few enthusiasts may do to promote a more meaningful worship or a more authentic Catholic witness in the world, so long as these efforts do not interfere with the Church's essentially protective role toward both her institutions and her members; that the calling of the Second Vatican Council has created a new climate. As far as we laymen are concerned, we must resign ourselves to submit to the essentially protective role of the Church toward both her institutions and her members; this will always be, and it need not, by any means, be a detriment.

She says further: "The role of the Church, therefore, is now clearly not so much to protect as to communicate—to communicate Christ's truth and life to her members and, through them, to all of human society. It is not so much to conserve as to grow—to 'grow up in all things in Christ, by doing the truth in love.' It is not to keep its members safe, but to open out to them in all its urgency Christ's invitation to lose their lives in order to find them. It is not to protect itself from a hostile world, but to go out to proclaim the Good News in word and life and to make Good News credible by the witness of Christian love."

I cannot believe that this point of view is entirely new. Some of this spirit has always existed, and to a different extent in different places and with different people. To be sure, it has been given greater emphasis and pro-pulsion in recent times, but it has always been necessary to carry it on with great circumspec-tion. Certainly, we cannot go out among our non-Catholic friends and ram the Good News down their throats, whether they wish it or not. And there will still be a great many who will not wish it.

Before taking up the conclusions reached by Mrs. Ryan, I would like to state some of my own, and unequivocally so. It seems to me, first of all, that we must have a thorough knowledge of what Catholic education is. It cannot be a single, simple system applicable to every section of the country and quite inflexi-ble in nature. Its nature and aims must be un-

65

changing and the same for all, but local conditions and availability of resources will require variations of implementation.

The unchanging picture, I think most Catholic educators would agree, should be very much as I have described it in the first part of this discussion. Toward this goal, all diocesan school systems and individual Catholic educators should strive. Lack of resources, especially too few teachers and inadequate buildings, will cause, in the wisdom of those in charge, the elimination of certain grades, either at the beginning or the top of the system, or the introduction of a program of part-time or short-time or released-time instruction in the public schools, or any similar device, but all this should be on a strictly temporary basis, looking forward to the abandonment of more and more of these transient measures as our increasing resources permit. But our ideal must never be lost sight of.

The public schools should be a cause of great concern to all good Americans. Certainly, as good Americans, we wish our public system to grow and prosper. The country needs them for its own future welfare. They will be of benefit to all Americans whether they all wish

PART II

to make immediate use of them or not. No worthy American should refer to them as some used to do in the past, as "Godless Schools," "Secular Education" with a derogatory emphasis on the word "secular," and similar expressions. That they would ever be "reduced to comparative unimportance," as Mrs. Ryan suggests, seems ridiculous to me.

Mrs. Ryan's question as to whether a Catholic public, still wedded to the concept that only religious can **really** provide a Catholic education, would welcome or support schools largely staffed by laity, is a purely academic one. The graduates of the several Catholic colleges for women in and around Washington definitely do not want to teach in Catholic schools. They not only apply for jobs in public schools, but are regularly accepted for these positions. In spite of their numbers, let no one think that they represent any force for the spread of Catholicism. They are regularly carefully watched for any possible proselitising and, furthermore, I doubt that any one of them ever thinks in those terms. Moreover, only a few Catholic parents object to members of the laity teaching their children in Catholic schools, and then only when these laymen are distinctly incompetent, and, of course, this happens all too often. Of this, I am most certain.

There are several passages in the last chapter which I would like to discuss, but space will not permit. I would, however, like to bring up a very good point. The author says: "In trying to provide a total Catholic education for as many of our young people as possible, we have been neglecting to provide anything like adequate **religious** formation for all those not in Catholic schools, and we have been neglecting the religious formation of adults." Some efforts have been made in these directions, but, by no means, enough and not as much as can be done. Some dioceses, the Archdiocese of Washington for example, conducts an annual retreat for Catholic students in the public schools, also a well developed CCD program. This practice is fairly widespread. Perhaps more along this line could be done. Regarding adults, far too little and not enough of the proper kind of instruction is being carried out. I myself have called attention to this within my own University, and, in general, within my recent publications. Surely, the work which needs to be done within this area is not fully appreciated by Catholic educators, or, if it is realized, very little action has been taken concerning it.

The very last paragraph of this book is the most shocking. It is both intemperate and not at all in accordance with an understanding of the facts.

Mrs. Ryan says that we are called to witness to Christ and to His presence and activity in His Church on every level and in every aspect of our society, and that we only carry out this work, first, by putting ourselves, and by helping to put one another, in as close contact as possible with the Christ who speaks to us and acts on us in His Word, in the sacrifice and sacraments of the Church, and then by putting ourselves in contact with our neighbor, sharing his interests and concerns, working with him for the welfare of all men. **It is hard to see how, under present circumstances, the continuance or the extension of the Catholic school system can be anything but an obstacle to the pursuit of these aims.** I cannot see how Mrs. Ryan can fully understand and be aware of the activity of the Catholic school system, and make such a damaging statement as this. The Catholic school system has its weaknesses, but these we should be glad to have pointed out to us. More-

NATURE OF CATHOLIC EDUCATION

over, we should make every effort to strengthen these weaknesses. But let us never forget what the system has done in the past and is continuing to do. Above all things, let us not forget what the true meaning of Catholic education is and let us carry it out on all levels of education as far as resources permit. God help the Catholic Church in the United States, if we abandon the Catholic school system.

I have, by no means, touched upon all the statements in Mrs. Ryan's book that might well be refuted. Only a small number, as representative, have been presented.

Knowing Mrs. Ryan as I do, I can only say that it is unfortunate that she ever wrote such a book as "Are Parochial Schools the Answer?" I do not, for a moment, question her sincerity and interest in the cause of Catholic education. I feel that she did not consult the right people in the course of her labors, and perhaps unconsciously sought approval for certain impressions which, if she had investigated them in a scholarly and objective manner, she would not have continued to hold. Question might also be seriously raised as to her competence by reason of her previous training and experience to carry on such an important study. The fact that Mrs. Ryan has raised five children of her own, as laudable as that may be, does not give her the background necessary to discuss such a subject as "Are Parochial Schools the Answer?". Yet I feel that if she had attempted to bring out wherein Catholic education is failing, while at the same time recognizing the good that it has accomplished and the progress that it is making, in other words, with a full understanding of the philosophy of Catholic education and an objective, not impressionistic, knowledge of its present status, much benefit would have been derived from her work. As it is, I fear that some harm, at least temporarily, will be done to the Catholic school system.

NOTES TO PART II

[1] Cf. St. Thomas and St. Augustine as quoted in Part I.

[2] Cf. *Affiliation Bulletin on Secondary Education,* Series XXV, no. 4, "Fringe Benefits for the Lay Teacher in Catholic Schools," by Rita Watrin.

ABOUT THE AUTHOR

Dr. Roy Joseph Deferrari Ph.D., scholar, educator and author, has an outstanding reputation in the field of Catholic education. He was born in Stoneham, Massachusetts in 1890. In 1912 he received his Bachelor's Degree from Dartmouth College. P r i n c e t o n University awarded him his Master's Degree in 1913 and his Ph.D. in 1915. After serving in the 814th Aero Squadron in 1917-18, Dr. Deferrari joined the faculty of the Catholic University of America on December 9, 1918. His wise leadership and keen foresight were instrumental in making the Catholic University one of the foremost institutions in higher education in the United States.

Dr. Deferrari holds honorary degrees from various colleges and universities. He was made a Knight of Sylvester by His Holiness Pope John XXIII in 1959 and received the St. John Baptist de la Salle Medal from Manhatten College in 1960.

Dr. Deferrari has written widely on the field of higher education and is editor of the C.U.A. Patristic Series, Medieval Latin Series, Fathers of the Church, Inc., and numerous other publications. He has also authored such books as a **Complete Index of the Summa Theologica of St. Thomas Aquinas,** and a **Latin English Dictionary of St. Thomas Aquinas.**

DAUGHTERS OF ST. PAUL,

In Massachusetts
50 St. Paul's Avenue
Jamaica Plain,
Boston 30, Mass.
172 Tremont St.,
Boston 11, Mass.
381 Dorchester St.
So. Boston 27, Mass.
325 Main St.
Fitchburg, Mass.

In New York
78 Fort Place,
Staten Island 1, N.Y.
39 Erie St.,
Buffalo 2, N.Y.
625 East 187th Street
Bronx, N.Y.

In Connecticut
202 Fairfield Ave.,
Bridgeport, Conn.

In Ohio
141 West Rayen Ave.,
Youngstown 3, Ohio
Cleveland, Ohio

In Texas
114 East Main Plaza,
San Antonio 5, Texas

In California
1570 Fifth Ave.,
San Diego 1, Calif.

In Florida
2700 Biscayne Blvd.
Miami 37, Florida

In Louisiana
86 Bolton Ave.,
Alexandria, La.

In Canada
8885 Blvd. Lacordaire,
St. Leonard Deport-Maurice,
Montreal, Canada
1063 St. Clair Ave. West,
Toronto, Canada

In England
29 Beauchamp Place,
London, S.W. 3, England

In Africa
Box 4392
Kampala, Uganda

In India
Water Field Road Extension,
Plot N. 143,
Bandra, India

In Philippine Islands
No. 326 Lipa City,
Philippine Islands

In Australia
58 Abbotsford Rd.,
Homebush N.S.W., Australia